"Reading opens new doors to the world"

This
Book was
generously
donated to
St. Margaret
Middle School
by

The Taylor
Family, 2001

D1063940

The history of emigration from

SCOTLAND

Mike Hirst

FRANKLIN WATTS

A Division of Grolier Publishing

NEW YORK • LONDON • HONG KONG • SYDNEY

DANBURY, CONNECTICUT

Franklin Watts
A Division of Grolier Publishing Co., Inc.
Sherman Turnpike
Danbury, Connecticut 06813

Library of Congress Cataloging-in-Publication Data
Hirst, Mike.
    Scotland/by Mike Hirst.
        p. cm. --(Origins)
    Includes index.
    Summary: Discusses the history of emigration
from Scotland, detailing accounts of the migrants'
experiences and emphasizing their positive input to
new countries.
    ISBN 0-531-14441-0
    1. Scotland--Emigration and immigration--
History--Juvenile literature. 2. Scots--Foreign
countries--History--Juvenile literature. [1. Scotland-
-Emigration and immigration.] I. Title. II. Series:
Origins (New York, N.Y.)
DA774.5H57 1997
304.8'09411--dc20   96-44934
                               CIP
                               AC

Editor: Sarah Snashall
Series editor: Rachel Cooke
Designer: Simon Borrough
Picture research: Sarah Moule

Printed in Malaysia

Picture acknowledgements
t=top; b=bottom; m=middle; r=right; l=left
e. t. archive pp. 23t, 24(t and b)
AKG pp. 6b (Erich Lessing), 26t, 28t
Bridgeman Art Library pp. 5 (Eugene Deveria,
Chief of a Scottish Clan, City of Edinburgh
Museums and Art Galleries), 10t (Rosa
Bonheur, *The Highland Shepherd*, Bury Art
Gallery and Museum, Lancashire), 14t
(Smithsonian Institution, Washington D.C.),
16 (C. F. Ulrich, *In the Land of Promise*,
Corcoran Gallery of Art, Washington D.C.),
19t (Thomas Faed, *Scottish Settlers in North
America*, Haworth Art Gallery, Accrington,
Lancashire), 20t (W. Alsworth, *The
Emigrants*, National Library of Australia,
Canberra)
Canadian Tourist Office p. 29(both)
Mary Evans pp. 21b, 25t
Robert Harding pp. 4(main), 7 (Michael
Jenner), 8b (Roy Rainford), 12b, 23b
Hulton Getty pp. 3, 10b, 11, 14b, 15, 17, 19b,
20b, 21t, 22(both), 25b
Image Select pp. 6t, 18t
A F Kersting p. 28b
Mansell Collection pp. 8t, 12t, 13, 24m
Rex Features pp. 4l, 18b (J. Sutton-Hibbert), 27
Scottish National Portrait Gallery p. 9
map p.4 Julian Baker

Contents

"A Spirit of Emigration"

"There is a spirit of emigration in this country ... that is close to madness."

In 1774, a customs officer in the Scottish port of Wigtown wrote, "There is a spirit of emigration in this country ... that is close to madness." In 1774–75, 2,773 Scots left Scotland to settle in North America. These early emigrants were only the beginning of a huge movement of Scottish people. Over the next two centuries, "the spirit of emigration" would take not thousands, but millions of Scots as far afield as Canada, the United States, Australia, and New Zealand.

▶ The country of Scotland includes the Highlands, the Lowlands, and over 800 islands off its western and northern coasts.

In the Highlands (above), much of the land is too windswept and mountainous to grow crops, but the Lowlands (below) have rich farmland.

Between 1774 and 1939, two and a half million Scots moved to new homes overseas. This was an enormous number for such a small country; even by 1939, the total population of Scotland was only five million people, and in 1801 it had been barely one and a half million. Why did so many Scots choose to emigrate? This book explains some of the reasons why, and how Scottish emigrants helped to shape the destinies of the new countries in which they settled.

The Scottish homeland

Scotland forms the northernmost part of the British Isles and has been part of the United Kingdom since 1707.

Today, most Scots live in an area called the Lowlands, which contains the best farming land and the two main cities of Glasgow and Edinburgh. The Northwest of Scotland is called the Highlands; here the land is rough and hilly, with wide stretches of moorland cut up by deep, narrow valleys known as glens or straths. Off the coast are hundreds of islands: the Inner and Outer Hebrides off the west coast and the Orkney and Shetland Islands to the north.

Highlanders and Lowlanders

Lowlanders have always had most contact with their English neighbors. There is no natural border between the countries, and as early as 1300 most Lowlanders already spoke a dialect of English (called Scots). There has been in the past, and remains in the present, a natural path of communication south of the border to England.

The way of life in the Highlands, however, was quite distinct from that in both England and the Lowlands. Living in isolated glens, far from the nearest roads, Highlanders spoke Gaelic and lived in clans, which were tribes made up of related families. The clan chiefs were often the virtual rulers of the Highland areas in which they lived. The distinct nature of these tight-knit communities affected the way the Highlanders were to emigrate: often leaving in large groups to settle abroad together.

▲ The Highland clans were ruled by powerful chiefs; this chief is carrying at least two swords, and has a fox fur at his belt and feathers in his cap which show his skill as a hunter.

The Plantation of Ulster

▲ Ireland had originally been ruled by Irish chieftains (above). English monarchs had been trying to govern Ireland for centuries, but the Irish chieftains often rose up against them.

◄ James VI and I had first tried out his scheme of plantation in Scotland, where he wanted to settle Lowland Scots in the Highlands, to increase his control over areas that were dominated by clan chieftains. In fact, these Highland plantations were far less successful than the Scottish and English colonies in Ulster.

Although the greatest emigrations from Scotland have taken place during the last 250 years, the first large movement of Scots began as early as 1610, and happened within the British Isles, when closer links were formed between Scotland, England, and Ireland.

The Scottish Reformation

In 1567, the Scottish parliament forced Scotland's queen, Mary, to abdicate (give up the throne) because she was a Catholic. Her young son, James VI, was declared king instead and raised as a Protestant. In 1603, Queen Elizabeth I of England died. James VI was Elizabeth's closest Protestant relation and was declared James I of England.

James VI and Ireland

Soon after James came to the English throne, there was an uprising of Irish chieftains or earls in the north of Ireland, an area known as Ulster. The earls were defeated by the English, and the leaders of the rebellion fled abroad. James then devised a scheme to bring Ulster under English control.

Scottish settlers left their mark on Ulster in many different ways. They introduced a Scottish style of castle-building, with distinctive round towers that are common in Scotland and Ulster, but rare in other parts of the British Isles.

The scheme for plantation

The English siezed the estates belonging to the Irish earls and offered their land instead to hundreds of "civil, loyal and dutiful subjects" from England and Scotland. These "dutiful subjects" would have the job of setting up farms and turning Ulster into a loyal colony of Scottish and English settlers. This was known as the plantation of Ulster.

The plantation began in 1609. First, the siezed land was parceled out into large estates. These estates were then granted to 51 English and 59 Scottish "undertakers."

The new landowners were called undertakers because they undertook to satisfy certain conditions of ownership. Each landowner had to bring a particular number of small farmers (called undertenants or cottagers) across to Ireland to do the actual work on the land. On their estates, they also had to build stone houses and bawns (defensible courtyards with strong walls), where cattle could be herded during an attack.

The plantation flourishes

By 1619, the plantation was well under way. There were 107 castles with bawns, and many of the estates already had the required number of English or Scottish settlers. New towns were formed, and other settlers such as merchants, peddlers, blacksmiths, and shipwrights moved to Ireland alongside the farmers. Scottish settlers seem to have been particularly successful, and by 1638, there were probably about 40,000 Scots in Ireland. The Scots were skilled farmers, as one survey of Ulster conducted in 1619 pointed out:

"Many English do not yet plough, nor use husbandry, being fearful to stock themselves with cattle or servants for these labours . . . were it not for the Scottish, who plough in many places, the rest of the country might starve."

▲ One of the effects of the plantation was that Ulster became a focus of the conflict between Catholics and Protestants. In 1685, King James II of England and VII of Scotland was out of favor because he had become a Catholic. In 1689, he lay siege to Londonderry in an attempt to retain his crown. Major General Kirk (above) defeated the King and the Protestant William of Orange succeeded James to the throne.

Emigration from Scotland continued to take place, particularly during the 1690s, when Scotland itself suffered from crop failures and food shortages. By 1700 there were about 100,000 Scots living in Ulster—a large number when the entire population of Scotland was only about one million.

Ulster today

The migration of Scots (and, to a lesser extent, the English) to Ulster left its mark on Northern Ireland. Most of the Scottish and English settlers were Protestant. This contrasted with the rest of Ireland, which was Catholic.

Today, the mixed population of Catholics and Protestants has created political problems in Northern Ireland. When Ireland gained its independence from Britain in 1923, Protestants in the north wanted to remain part of the United Kingdom, and Ulster actually stayed within the United Kingdom. In recent years, there has been bitter conflict between those people in Ulster who would like the province to join the rest of Ireland and those who wish to remain part of the United Kingdom.

► Londonderry was founded at the time of the plantation by several London merchants' companies. However, it quickly became a town peopled by Scottish settlers, as it was the most convenient port in Ulster for sailings to and from Scotland.

Changes in the Highlands

"The dance seems intended to show how emigration catches, till a whole neighbourhood is set afloat."

In 1700, most Highlanders still lived in their traditional clans, farming land in the glens together and grazing cattle on common moorland pasture. Rent was paid to a middle-ranking landlord called a tacksman, who controlled a section of the clan chief's territory.

The tacksman was also responsible for supplying his chief with a regular supply of fighting men. Modern law and order was virtually unknown in the Highlands, and clan chiefs were all-powerful. Yet within 100 years, this way of life had disappeared entirely and many Highlanders had left Scotland altogether.

New roads, built after the Jacobite uprising of 1715 by the English General Wade (above), were vital in opening up the Highlands to new influences and ways of life.

The Jacobite rebellions

One of the reasons for the change in Highland life lay in the Jacobite rebellions. In 1707, the Act of Union had formally joined England and Scotland. Yet many Scots still wanted their country to be independent. In 1715, and again in 1745, groups of Scots rose up unsuccessfully against the English and tried to put an independent Scottish king on the Scottish throne. In response, the government in London took measures which would help it to control the Highlands more closely.

Highlanders were forbidden to carry weapons and, for a time, even to wear the traditional tartan cloth that was the mark of their clan. Lands owned by the chiefs who had supported the rebellions were taken over.

Sheep and crofting

At the same time, clan chiefs themselves introduced new ways of farming. They no longer needed tacksmen to recruit large private armies, so they began to take direct control of their own land. Clan members were moved to small individual plots of land, called crofts. They now paid rents straight to the chief, or landowner, and were no longer allowed to graze their cattle on the common land. As time went on, more and more landowners would put these wide tracts of open moorland to a new and more profitable use—sheep farming.

"A dance called America"

As early as the 1730s, Highlanders were already beginning to seek a new life abroad rather than stay in the crofting townships that had been formed following the breakdown of the old clan system. At first, many Scots sailed for the North American colony of North Carolina.

This emigration was often led by tacksmen, who were in danger of losing their status and influence if they remained in Scotland. They often took with them many

▲ From the mid 1700s onwards, sheep farming became more and more common in the Highlands.

▶ One way for the British government to pacify the Highlands was to recruit Highlanders into the British Army. Special regiments of Highland soldiers, such as the 42nd Highland Watch, were founded after 1715.

ordinary clan members, who were worried about having to pay more rent to farm their land in Scotland. When a tacksman decided to emigrate, it was common for him to pin a notice on the church door, asking if any of his clan members wanted to accompany him. For example, in 1774 James Hogg, a tacksman from Caithness, led a party of 280 people to North Carolina.

Emigration became infectious across the Highlands. In 1785, James Boswell wrote the following:

"In the evening, we performed a dance which, I suppose, the emigration from Skye has occasioned. They call it America. Each of the couples ... whirls round in a circle till all are in motion; and the dance seems intended to show how emigration catches, till a whole neighbourhood is set afloat."

We do not know exactly how many Highlanders emigrated during the 1700s, but shipping records do give us quite a good picture of who left Scotland and where they went. Certainly by the 1760s and early 1770s, the number of migrants in North Carolina—and the other North American colonies—were increasing dramatically. Probably about 2,000 Scots moved to North Carolina from 1768–72 alone.

▼ An emigration ship waits in the harbour of Cambelton on the Isle of Skye. The number of people on Skye has never reached the level it was at before emigration took hold in the 1700s.

Emigration after 1783

Highland emigration to North America came to a sudden standstill during the War of American Independence (1776–83). Emigration began again after the war, encouraged by a disastrous harvest in 1782, which left many Highland farmers worse off than ever.

However, in the years immediately after 1783, Highlanders tended to settle in those parts of North America that remained British and would later form the nation of Canada. Prince Edward Island and Nova Scotia were both popular destinations.

North to Canada

Other Highlanders, who had originally settled in the United States, moved farther north after American independence. Glengarry County in Ontario was founded by a group of Highlanders, originally from Glengarry, who had first moved to the Mohawk Valley (New York State) in 1773.

Wherever they went, these early Highland emigrants tended to stick together. By 1800, North America had many settlements of Highland clan members, living together in small farming communities in much the same way as they had back in Scotland.

But it was not necessarily an easy life, as one Highlander wrote from Nova Scotia:

> *"Before I make a clearing and raise crops and tear the forest up from its roots by the strength of my arms, I'll be worn out, and almost spent before my children grow up."*

▲ Parts of Canada contained rich, fertile farmland and offered great opportunities for Scottish settlers. Yet bringing this land under the plow involved years of hard work (top).

The Industrial Revolution

"To the West, to the West, to the land of the free, Where the mighty Missouri rolls down to the sea."

Slums developed in Glasgow in the mid 1900s as people flocked to the city to find work in the factories. Many Scots escaped this poverty by emigrating to America which itself was becoming industrialized.

Just as the Highlands experienced great changes in the 1700s, by 1800 life in the Lowlands was also being transformed. New factories and new industries was now making the Lowlands one of the most important industrial regions of Britain.

New factories, new towns

Among the new industries were linen and cotton mills, coal mines, and iron- and steel-works. Skilled engineers also made machines and machine tools, and on the Clyde estuary, Scottish shipyards built the world's biggest and most modern ships.

As industry expanded, so too did the population, and many Lowland towns grew rapidly in size. The largest city by far was Glasgow, a town of just 12,000 people in 1707 but that by the 1900s would have over a million inhabitants.

Winners and losers

Although the Industrial Revolution brought wealth to Scotland, it was by no means shared equally among everyone. Factory owners, tradespeople, and some skilled workers became richer, yet for unskilled factory workers, life was hard. They had to work long hours for low pay, and living conditions in the poor districts of Glasgow were squalid.

▲ The first cotton mill in the United States established at Pawtucket, Rhode Island in the late 18th century. Scottish cotton mill workers could take their skills to the U.S. where they received higher wages than at home.

▲ An American coal mine in the 19th century. Scottish workers also played a vital part in the development of the U.S. mining industry.

Pushes and pulls

When they look at migration, historians talk about two kinds of causes: pushes (the things that "push" people away from their homes) and pulls (the things that attract, or "pull" people to a new land). During the 1800s, Lowland Scots experienced both strong pushes and powerful pulls.

Poor conditions at home were an obvious push, especially when a group of people suddenly found themselves worse off than they had been before. Many hand-loom weavers emigrated during the 1820s, for instance, when new machine-operated power looms led to a drop in their wages. Emigration was also more common at times of high unemployment, such as just after the Napoleonic Wars, which ended in 1815.

Yet after 1815, the pulls also became ever more powerful, particularly the exciting opportunities offered by one rapidly developing country: the United States of America.

Scots in the United States of America

To many Scots, American industry offered better prospects and higher wages. By 1850, it was said that wages in the United States were 50 percent higher than in Scotland, while food prices were 30 percent lower.

Many Scottish immigrants were to be found working in, and even controlling, American factories. James Montgomery, for instance, founded a U.S. cotton factory in 1836, while the manager of the Singer sewing-machine company was George Mackenzie.

The skills of Scottish engineers, iron- and steel-workers, papermakers, shipbuilders, stone masons and coal miners were all desperately needed in the United States. Particularly in Illinois and Iowa, many coal mines were worked by Scots.

Beginning to integrate

Groups of people from the Lowlands often traveled together to North America and even settled together in the same places, but they formed fewer new, specifically "Scottish" settlements than the Highlanders. Instead of founding farming communities, they tended to work in large towns and cities, with neighbors and fellow workers from a whole variety of other European countries.

When Lowlanders were successful in North America, they would often send glowing reports back to Scotland, which in turn encouraged more emigrants.

Opportunities to work on the new railroads were an important pull to North America after the 1840s.

"To the land of the free"

The United States also appealed to some Scottish workers because it seemed to be a fairer, more equal society. In Britain, the Chartist movement of the 1830s and 1840s had struggled to get the vote for ordinary workers, but their demands were rejected by a government elected by the middle and upper classes. Emigration often appealed to Scottish radicals in search of a freer, more democratic home; one verse chanted by Chartists went:

In spite of the pulls to a better life in North America, emigration was never easy, and life for unskilled workers in the United States could be just as difficult as back in Europe. This painting is called, "In the Land of Promise"— emigration abroad did not always fulfill dreams of wealth and happiness.

"To the West, to the West, to the land of the free,
Where the mighty Missouri rolls down to the sea;
Where a man is a man even though he must toil,
And the poorest may gather the fruits of the soil."

Other influences on emigration

Initially, the British government had opposed emigration because of the drain of labor, but, as the British population grew, governments changed their attitude. By 1825, the government was actually encouraging the emigration of poor and unemployed people, and from 1815 onward it supported local emigration societies.

Shipping companies also encouraged emigration, and by the mid-1800s century, carrying people to North America was big business. In their advertisements, companies drew a rosy picture of an emigrant's prospects. It was even said that one group of emigrants in 1801 had been told that in North America they would find trees that bore soap and sugar and that the continent was only a short distance beyond the Western Isles. When they reached the Outer Hebrides, the travellers asked hopefully, "Is this America?"

The Highland Clearances

Crofting never made Highlanders rich, but as the 1800s went on, scenes of poverty such as this became more and more common in the crofting communities.

"If the potatoes continue to fail, the inhabitants of Lewis cannot be made self-sustaining unless a considerable number of them remove elsewhere."

For a time toward the end of the late 1700s, it looked as though crofting might provide a decent living for ordinary Highlanders. They began to cultivate a new crop, the potato, which grew so well that even a small croft could produce enough food to feed a family. Highlanders also made money by fishing for herring, making whisky, and gathering kelp—a kind of seaweed that, when burned, produces soda used to manufacture soap and glass.

The failure of crofting

Unfortunately, by 1815 the weaknesses of the crofting system were becoming all too obvious. As families grew, crofts were split up between children. The plots of farmland became smaller than ever, and crofters became poorer. A cheap chemical substitute for kelp was invented, and herring fishing proved to be very unreliable. Crofters found it increasingly difficult to pay their rents.

At the same time, sheep farming became more profitable, as Scotland's growing towns and cities demanded mutton to eat, and textile mills needed wool to make into cloth. Gradually, crofters began to be turned off their land to make way for more sheep.

▲ Potato blight
(*Phytophtera
infestans*) devastated
the Scottish potato
crop in 1846.

▼ The landscape of
the Highlands is still
dotted with crofts
abandoned during
the clearances.

The clearances

The process of evicting crofters from their land is known as the Highland clearances. It was already under way well before 1800, and by the mid-1800s, thousands of acres had already been cleared by large landowners—some of them the descendants of the old clan chiefs, others wealthy southerners who had bought the land recently.

On the Duchess of Sutherland's estate alone, 10,000 people were moved out between 1807 and 1821. In some cases, people's homes were burned to the ground before their very eyes to stop them from going back to their crofts. Many Sutherlanders then chose to go abroad rather than settle in other parts of Scotland, and emigration from the Highlands was common throughout the 1820s and 1830s. However, the greatest upheaval was yet to come.

The potato blight

In 1845, the potato crop throughout much of Europe was affected by a terrible new disease known as potato blight. In 1846, this disease reached the Highlands. Many crofters fell behind with their rents, and suffered terrible sickness and malnutrition. The local authorities had to form boards of poor relief to prevent the small farmers from starving.

Some Highlanders decided to leave Scotland and could afford the cost of a passage to North America, but most of the destitute crofters were too poor to pay for their own emigration.

"Assisted emigration"

Faced with having to provide relief for the starving crofters on their estates, many landowners chose to send their poor abroad. The British government helped the landowners with cheap loans, and between 1846 and 1857, thousands of Highlanders, mainly from the Hebrides and northwestern mainland, were sent to North America this way.

On the island of Lewis, for instance, almost 2,500 people (about 14 percent of the total population) were "helped" to emigrate. The landowner, James Matheson, canceled their debts, paid their passages, bought up their cattle and other goods at the going rate, and paid the wages of a minister to accompany them. Yet any who refused to leave quietly were evicted from their land, and their crofts burned down.

▼ Scottish settlers in North America. Life often remained hard for the Scottish settlers who had been helped to emigrate, sometimes against their wishes, to North America.

The Highlands and Islands Emigration Society

Even with government help, some landowners on the Isle of Skye were too "financially embarrassed" to send their tenants overseas. Here, emigration was encouraged by a charity, the Highlands and Islands Emigration Society, founded by Sir Charles Trevelyan in 1852. Trevelyan had been in charge of British famine relief in Ireland, which was also devastated by the potato blight, and he was convinced that "the only immediate remedy for the present state of things in Skye is emigration." However, Trevelyan's society concentrated on sending emigrants not to North America but yet farther afield, to Australia.

▼ Melbourne harbour, the place where many of the settlers, sent abroad by the Highlands and Islands Emigration Society, first set foot on Australian soil.

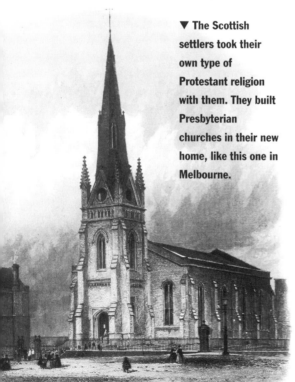

▲ Scottish settlers in Australia in the mid 1800s; the prosperity that Australia seemed to offer was a strong pull for many Scots.

▼ The Scottish settlers took their own type of Protestant religion with them. They built Presbyterian churches in their new home, like this one in Melbourne.

Immigration to Australia

The first Englishman to visit Australia was Captain James Cook in 1770. He declared it a British colony, but for many years, it attracted few settlers. The voyage to Australia was long and hard, often lasting six months, and at first the only Europeans there were British criminals who had been shipped out to penal colonies.

Yet by the 1830s, settlers were going to Australia of their own free will. The country was particularly attractive to Scots because it offered opportunities for sheep and cattle farming. The Australian Company of Edinburgh began regular sailings to New South Wales in 1822, and by 1839, Melbourne was described as "a Scotch colony." One settler in Adelaide wrote in 1847, "This country is replete with plenty. Here is no starvation, no seizing of your goods for taxes, no begging for work."

The greatest boost to Australian immigration came in 1851, when gold was discovered. Men rushed to the gold fields, both from within Australia and from overseas.

Many Scottish settlers went to seek their fortunes in the gold fields of Australia.

However, the Highlands and Islands Emigration Society concentrated on sending families to Australia to populate settled, long-term farming communities. Yorkshire mill owners—and Queen Victoria—supported the society in this policy because they feared a wool shortage if too many of the existing Australian farmers abandoned their land to look for gold. Between 1852 and 1857, the society helped 4,910 Scots travel to Australia.

Highland emigration: a necessary evil?

The Highland clearances and assisted emigration are two of the most controversial events in Scottish history. At the time, some people believed that clearances were the work of hard-hearted, grasping landlords, who were too mean to look after their tenants in times of hardship. Others, however, thought that crofting would never offer the Highlanders a decent way of life and that clearance and emigration were necessary evils; they would make everyone—both landlords and crofters—better off in the long run.

A government servant, Sir John McNeill, stated the point of view of the Lewis landowners:

"I am clearly of the opinion that, if the potatoes continue to fail, the inhabitants of Lewis cannot be made self-sustaining unless a considerable number of them remove elsewhere."

▼ A swagman—or travelling laborer—tells traditional Australian stories to settler children in the mid 1800s.

▶ However difficult conditions became in the Highlands, some crofters refused to emigrate abroad because of their fears about the long voyage in cramped, unhealthy conditions.

▼ Ballads such as this were one way for emigrants to express their homesickness.

A tough choice

Yet emigration was not an easy solution, and many Highlanders did not want to leave. The voyage was uncomfortable and dangerous—it was normal for at least 3 percent of passengers to die on board any emigrant ship from anywhere in Europe—and most emigrants had no clear idea how they would support themselves when they arrived.

In any event, few Highlanders had any real choice about leaving their homes. Evictions were generally carried out ruthlessly. Angus Cameron described how one old woman would not leave her croft until it had been set on fire:

> *"I got my hands burnt taking out the poor old woman from amidst the flames of her once comfortable though humble dwelling . . .[she uttered] piercing moans of distress and agony, in articulation of which could only be understood, 'Oh Dhia, Dhia, teine, teine' ('Oh God, God, fire, fire')."*

In one respect, the Highlanders were fortunate. The potato blight occurred at a time when the colonies were ready to welcome large numbers of immigrants. Australian farming was just taking off, and in Canada, a boom in railway building meant that there was plenty work for unskilled laborers.

Scots Throughout the Empire

Scottish civil servants, engineers, and army officers were vital to the control and development of the British colonies.

No Scottish communities were disturbed as violently in the mid-1800s as the Highland crofting townships. Yet even when the clearances became less frequent, after 1860, emigration from Scotland as a whole continued to increase.

Between 1860 and 1909, the United States was the most popular destination for Scots. Two other new colonies also welcomed Scottish immigrants.

New Zealand and South Africa

New Zealand became a British colony in 1840 and, with its opportunities for sheep farming, attracted many Scots. The most "Scottish" part of the colony was in Otago, on South Island. There, Presbyterian Scots (who belonged to a strict Protestant sect) modeled the city of Dunedin on Edinburgh.

There was a good living to be made in New Zealand. Sheep farming had flourished: the invention of refrigerator ships, to transport frozen meat, meant that mutton as well as wool could be exported. A gold rush in the 1860s attracted even more migrants, and Scots continued to settle in New Zealand for the rest of the century.

▲ Dunedin in New Zealand has a Princes Street and a Canongate just like Edinburgh on which it was modeled. Dunedin was the Celtic name for Edinburgh.

▼ Sheep farming remains an important part of New Zealand's economy today.

South Africa opened up to British settlers later than most other colonies, when much of the country's farmland had already been taken by earlier Dutch settlers. After the discovery of gold and diamonds, however, Scots did immigrate to South Africa, often to work as engineers in the mines or other growing industries.

▲ Diamond mining brought not only Scottish laborers to South Africa, but also Scottish engineers, doctors, and bankers.

Explorers, traders, and civil servants

By the late 1800s, century the British Empire had reached its greatest extent. Britain ruled over huge areas of land, especially in Asia and Africa. Many parts of this empire, such as India and Nigeria, already had large native populations and did not attract British emigrants in the same way as Canada and Australia. Yet, alongside other Britons, Scottish civil servants, engineers, and army officers were vital to the control and development of the British colonies. There were many career opportunities for Scots both in trade and the imperial civil service.

In fact, Scottish explorers played a crucial part in expanding the empire, and opening up new regions to British control. John Stuart, for example, was the first man to cross Australia from Adelaide to Darwin in 1861–62.

Some explorers were driven by a desire to preach Christianity to the native peoples of non-Christian countries. The Rev. R. Montgomery spoke to the Glasgow Society for the Extinction of the Slave Trade and for the Civilization of Africa:

"Instead of forest depths ... may the thronged city, the busy wharf, the crowded street hereafter be seen, with all the glow of commercial and social advancement. Instead of the clank of chains, there may be heard the voice of prayer, the sound of praise and the sweet music of the church-going bell."

▲ Missionary-explorer, David Livingstone. Victorian Britons regarded Livingstone as one of the greatest men of their age.

▼ British army officers and their wives photographed outside their home in India. The British civil service provided jobs for Scots throughout the British Empire.

The most famous missionary-explorer was David Livingstone (1813–73), who travelled widely in central southern Africa. Livingstone wanted to stamp out the African slave trade, and although he had some success in achieving this aim, his voyages opened up large areas of Zimbabwe and Zambia to a different kind of exploitation—economic exploitation by British traders and industrialists. Indeed, it was common for missionary activity and trade to go hand in hand. The African Lakes Company was founded by Glasgow merchants in 1878 "to advance the kingdom of God by honest trade."

Emigration in the 1900s

Emigration reached a peak in the first thirty years of the 1900s. After 1900, Canada once again became a popular destination, rivaling the United States. This was the time when settlers discovered that fertile farmland in the west of Canada could yield more corn per acre than any U.S. state.

The First World War (1914–18) brought emigration almost to a complete halt, but the 1920s saw another great

▲ Men stand in line at a job centre in the United States in 1938. The depression of the 1930s brought a virtual end to emigration from Scotland as fortunes ceased to be made abroad.

▼ This table shows the numbers of Scots who emigrated to different parts of the world between 1830 and 1939.

wave of migration, both to the USA and within the British Empire. Conditions for many working-class Scots were hard and in the 1920s, 8 percent of the entire Scottish population emigrated—compared with just 0.5 percent of the population of England and Wales. In addition, a great many Scots must have moved south of the border to England during the early 1900s; in 1931 over 350,000 people living in England had been born in Scotland.

Emigration ends

However, emigration trailed off suddenly after 1930, when the world economy was hit by the depression. Unemployment and poverty increased dramatically in Scotland, but, if anything, conditions were worse in North America. There was now no point in emigrating.

Emigration to Canada and Australia, supported by the governments of those countries, picked up for a while after the Second World War (1939–45). However, the "pushes" towards emigration grew weaker in the late 1950s as the whole of Britain entered a period of increased prosperity and low unemployment.

Emigration from Scotland (to nearest 100), 1830-1939

Years	United States	Canada	Australia New Zealand	South Africa
1830-39	16,200	40,900	7,700	–
1840-49	34,400	43,600	8,800	–
1850-59	66,000	42,200	48,200	–
1860-69	60,200	21,900	45,100	–
1870-79	90,200	26,100	40,200	–
1880-89	178,800	36,000	45,700	7,600
1890-99	120,700	17,300	13,900	19,900
1900-09	174,700	134,000	25,800	44,800
1910-14	95,300	168,300	44,800	15,500
1915-19	10,300	14,500	4,100	2,200
1920-29	158,200	174,700	90,100	15,000
1930-39	16,200	15,214	6,800	6,100

The Scots Abroad

In 1941, 10,000 residents of Cape Breton Island still gave Gaelic as their mother tongue.

Visitors to most major cities in North America, Australia, or Britain will see evidence of immigration from all around the world. But the descendants of Scottish immigrants are rarely as visible as other ethnic groups for various reasons.

Integration abroad

Large-scale Scottish emigration to North America and Australia was over by the Second World War and two or three generations have passed since the last great wave of Scottish immigrants entered these countries. Over the years, people with Scottish ancestry have mixed with their neighbors from other backgrounds and their "Scottishness" has become more and more diluted.

Moreover, the Scots have always found it comparatively easy to blend into their host countries. All Scottish emigrants were Christians, and after about 1860, by far the greatest majority of them were English-speaking, too. As almost all settled in countries where English was the dominant language and Christianity the dominant religion, the Scots found it much easier to assimilate than, say, Chinese-speaking Buddhists.

▼ Golf is one of Scotland's greatest and most popular cultural exports. Today it is played around the world.

Leaving a mark

However, the Scots have left their own distinctive mark on their host countries. The influences of Scottish immigrants can still be felt today in all the countries discussed in this book. Most obviously, there are families and places with Scottish names scattered throughout the English-speaking world. There is a Perth in Australia, a New Glasgow in Nova Scotia, Canada and an Inverdoon in South Africa. The name Nova Scotia, itself, is Latin for "new Scotland."

Wherever they went, Scots also took with them their own particular brand of Protestantism, called Presbyterianism, and many countries still have flourishing Presbyterian churches which Scots founded. In New Zealand, for instance, 18 percent of the population today is Presbyterian.

The strongest ties with traditional Scottish ways of life were kept by the settlements of Highlanders in eastern Canada. In Nova Scotia and Prince Edward Island, some clan members lived together in close-knit crofting communities long after crofting had virtually disappeared in Scotland itself. Gaelic survived longest in these areas, and in 1941, 10,000 residents of Cape Breton Island still gave Gaelic as their mother tongue.

▲ Andrew Carnegie left Scotland aged 13 in 1848. He amassed an enormous fortune through building railways and in the iron and steel industries. He later gave away about 350 million dollars, and is best known for founding free libraries.

▼ Dunedin University in New Zealand was based on Glasgow University in Scotland.

Scottish societies and associations

However, even in towns and cities, many descendants of Scottish immigrants have held on to their Scottish heritage. Often, Scottish culture and traditions are kept alive by Scottish societies. Such associations were originally intended as self-help organizations, with Scots who were already successfully settled, assisting newly arrived colonists, but today they are usually more like social clubs. Many of these societies are actually based on membership of the traditional clans (for example Clan Donald, for the decendants of the MacDonalds) and are connected by the Order of Scottish Clans. There are societies for each clan throughout the world.

These societies arrange a wide variety of cultural events. For example, they hold Burns Suppers (celebrating Scotland's best-known poet, Robert Burns). Hogmanay dinners are organized to celebrate New Year's Eve, traditionally a huge festival in Scotland itself. There are festivals of Highland dancing and music and Highland games at which people compete in specifically Scottish sports such as tossing the caber or curling. At these events, members can be seen playing the bagpipes and eating traditional Scottish foods such as haggis and oatcakes. The men may also wear traditional Highland dress—a tartan kilt.

Descendants of the Scottish settlers keep in touch with their Scottish roots by learning Scottish dances (above) or by visiting museums (below), like this one in Canada.

The spirit lives on

Even though they choose to celebrate their Scottish heritage, many of the descendants of 1800s Scottish emigrants never actually visit Scotland itself. Yet they can still feel proud of the achievements of their ancestors, who, often in difficult circumstances, carried their way of life to the four corners of the globe. In the words of the "Canadian Boat Song,"

> *"From the lone shieling of the misty island*
> *Mountains divide us, and the waste of seas—*
> *Yet still the blood is strong, the heart is Highland,*
> *As we in dreams behold the Hebrides."*

Timeline

1034 Most of southern Scotland is united as the Kingdom of the Scots.

1266 Western Isles become part of Scotland after defeat of their Viking overlords.

1414 First Scottish University is founded at St Andrews.

1469 Orkney and Shetland Islands transferred from Norway to Scotland.

1492 Christopher Columbus sails across Atlantic to the Caribbean, and becomes the first European in modern times to visit America.

1542 Mary Queen of Scots accedes to the throne.

1560 Scottish Reformation.

1567 Mary Queen of Scots abdicates; her infant son, James VI, becomes king.

1603 James VI of Scotland also becomes James I of England.

1609 Plans for the plantation of Ulster begin.

1616 Dutch explorers are the first Europeans to visit Australia.

1642 First European catches sight of New Zealand.

1707 Act of Union makes Scotland a part of the United Kingdom.

1715 First Jacobite rebellion is led by James Stuart.

1745 Second Jacobite rebellion led by Charles Stuart, "Bonnie Prince Charlie."

1770 Captain James Cook visits Australia and claims it as a colony for Britain.

1776–83 American War of Independence; thirteen North American colonies break away from Britain and form the United States.

1782 Emigration Act forbids British artisans to emigrate to the USA.

1803 Passenger Acts passed by British parliament to regulate and improve conditions on ships which transport emigrants to North America.

1800–15 Napoleonic Wars. Napoleon leads the French in a series of campaigns against other European powers. Napoleon is eventually defeated at Waterloo.

1825 Emigration Act repealed.

1847 Scottish potato blight.

1851 Australian gold rush begins.

1852 Highland and Islands Emigration Society founded.

1855 David Livingstone becomes the first European to visit the Victoria Falls on the Zambezi River.

1861–2 John Stuart crosses Australia from South to North.

1867 Dominion of Canada founded by the union of British provinces in North America.

1914–18 First World War.

1929 Wall Street Crash leads to a worldwide economic recession, with high unemployment in Europe and North America.

1939–45 Second World War.

Glossary

bawn: a word used in Northern Ireland to describe a walled enclosure where cattle (and people) could be gathered and protected in times of trouble.

Chartism: a British working-class movement in the 1830s and 40s. Chartists wanted various reforms; the most important was the right of all men to vote in general elections, regardless of how wealthy they were.

cholera: a disease carried through unclean water which causes diarrhea and severe dehydration. It was common in Britain until the late 1800s.

clan: from the Gaelic word clann, meaning "family." Highland clans were originally tribal groups of related families, who lived together in one particular region of the Highlands.

croft: a small farm, rented and run by just one family. Crofting became common in the Highlands after the break-up of the old clan system.

democratic: describes a system of government which is elected by the people, for the people. The more people who have the right to vote, the more democratic a country is thought to be.

Gaelic: the language (related to Irish and Welsh) spoken in Scotland before the introduction of English. Today, it is spoken in just a few parts of the Highlands.

glen: a deep, narrow valley in the Highland region, containing the best and most sheltered farmland.

Hogmanay: the Scottish name for New Year's Eve. Traditionally, Hogmanay is a big celebration in Scotland.

Industrial Revolution: the name used by historians to describe the huge changes in British industry during the years 1750–1850. The Industrial Revolution saw the growth of many new factories.

Jacobites: a group of Scottish rebels who wanted to break away from the union with England. They were called Jacobites because in 1715 they tried to put an independent Scottish king, James Stuart, on the Scottish throne; the Latin name for "James" is "Jacobus."

Lowlands: the low-lying region of central and eastern Scotland which contains most of the country's best farmland and its largest towns.

malnutrition: poor health due to not having enough good things to eat.

plantation: in this book, the colony of the English and Scottish settlers in Northern Ireland in the 1600s.

penal colonies: settlements in new countries used as prisons. In the 1800s, Britain sent prisoners to settlements in Australia instead of putting people in overcrowded prisons in Britain. The prisoners sent to the penal colonies in Australia were the first white people to settle there.

potato blight (*Phytophthora infestans*): a disease which attacks and kills potatoes. It spread rapidly through Europe in 1846–47, destroying almost the whole potato crop.

Presbyterian: a type of Protestant. Since the Reformation, Presbyterianism has been the dominant form of Protestant religion in Scotland.

Protestant: a type of Christian. In the 1500s, many Christians broke away from the authority of the Roman Catholic church and the Pope in Rome. These new kinds of non-Catholic Christians were called Protestants.

Reformation: the religious shake-up that took place in the 1500s. The Church of Scotland and the Church of England turned away from Catholicism and became Protestant.

shieling: a hut or shelter in the Highlands used by cattlemen or shepherds during the summer when their animals were grazing on the upland pastures.

strath: a glen

tacksman: the head man in a Highland village before the introduction of crofting. The tacksman collected rents for the clan chief, and had to provide the chief with warriors when he wanted to raid his neighbors or go to war.

tartan: a special kind of checked cloth woven and worn in the Highlands.

typhus: a disease spread by lice and causing fever, headaches and rashes.

United Kingdom: the collective name for the united countries of England, Scotland, and Wales, and the province of Northern Ireland.

Index